1st Grade
Enjoying God's Gifts

by Cherie Noel

Positive Action Bible Curriculum

1st Grade: Enjoying God's Gifts

First Edition Published 1990
Second Edition Published 2004

Printed in the United States of America

ISBN: 0-929784-44-9

Author: Cherie Noel
Curriculum Consultant: Helen Boen
Editors: Steve Braswell and Ben Wright
Layout and Design: Shannon Brown
Artwork: Julie Speer

Published by

Contents

Unit One • God's Gift: The World

The Story Of Creation

Lesson 1	Day And Night	7
Lesson 2	Sky, Plants, Sun, Moon And Stars	9
Lesson 3	God Makes Animals	13
Lesson 4	God Makes Man	15
Lesson 5	Work	17
Lesson 6	Rules	19

Unit Two • God's Gift: Special Promises

The Stories Of Noah, Abraham, Jacob And Joseph

Lesson 7	Noah Builds An Ark	22
Lesson 8	Abraham Obeys God	25
Lesson 9	Jacob Has A Dream	27
Lesson 10	Joseph Becomes A Leader	29

Unit Three • God's Gift: Worship

The Stories Of Josiah And Joash

Lesson 11	Josiah—The Boy King	33
Lesson 12	Josiah Reads God's Word	35
Lesson 13	Joash—The Boy Who Forgot God	37

Unit Four • God's Gift: A Savior

The Stories Of Jesus

Lesson 14	An Angel Visits Mary	43
Lesson 15	Jesus Is Born	45
Lesson 16	The Shepherds And The Wise Men	47
Lesson 17	The Boy Jesus	49
Lesson 18	Jesus Is Tempted	51
Lesson 19	Jesus Calls His Disciples	53
Lesson 20	Jesus Loves Children	55
Lesson 21	Jesus Feeds The 5,000	57
Lesson 22	Jesus Walks On The Water	59
Lesson 23	Jesus Heals A Blind Man	61
Lesson 24	The Lost Sheep	63
Lesson 25	Jesus Is Crucified	67
Lesson 26	Jesus Lives!	69

Unit Five • God's Gift: Children

The Story Of Samuel

Lesson 27	Hannah Prays For A Son	73
Lesson 28	God Speaks To Samuel	75

Unit Six • God's Gift: Friends

The Story Of David

Lesson 29	David Is Chosen As King	81
Lesson 30	David And Goliath	83
Lesson 31	David And Jonathan	85

Unit Seven • God's Gift: Special Blessings

The Story Of Elijah

Lesson 32	Elijah Helps Others	91
Lesson 33	Elijah Prays To God	93
Lesson 34	Elijah Goes To Heaven	95
Lesson 35	Let's Review	97

Unit One

God's Gift: The World

The Story of Creation

NASA

Lesson One

Day And Night

Use these words from Genesis 1:3 to fill in the blanks.
This is what God made on the first day.

God	light

God said, "Let there be light,"
and there was light.

Use these words to label the pictures.
These are things that were not here in the beginning.

people	animals	flowers	rivers

Label each picture with a word to tell what God made the third day.

Lesson Two

Sky, Plants, Sun, Moon And Stars

hill	tree	lake	plant	flower

God's Beautiful World

Make God's earth as beautiful as you can.
Finish the picture by drawing these things.

God's Gift: Four Seasons

Label the seasons.

summer	winter	spring	fall

Spring

Summer

fall

Winter